SCOOBI DOGE VIDEO

In "Scoobi Doge's Saga," the Etherik spaceship's crew, including a spectral Jihoz and visionary Vitalik Buterin, seeks the Moon's Bitecoin secrets.

This crypto-fueled adventure blends with unique ComicNFTs, and is backed by the memecoin $SCooBi, merging comics and blockchain in a community-driven narrative.

Source: youtube.com/watch?v=-mW4DMJMDbk

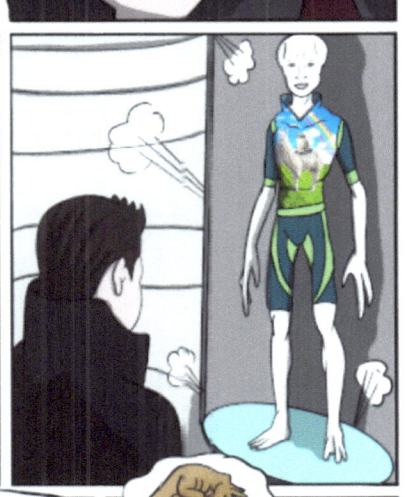

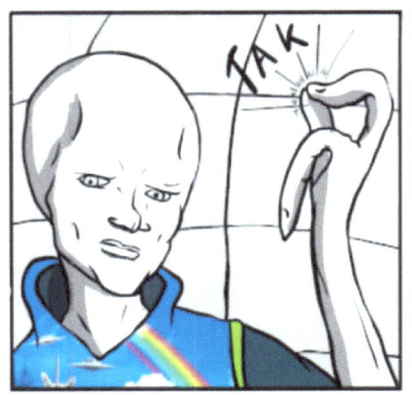

Jackie Ormes

This Comic Book is dedicated to the first Afro-American woman cartoonist in comics in history.

Jackie Ormes was born on August 1st of 1911 and died on December 26th, 1985 (aged 74). She was a proofreader in journalism and also worked as an editor and as a freelance writer, writing on police beats, court cases and human-interest topics. While she enjoyed "a great career running around town, looking into everything the law would allow, and writing about it," what she really wanted to do was draw.

SheOrmes's first comic strip, Torchy Brown in Dixie to Harlem, first appeared in the Pittsburgh Courier on May 1, 1937. Her work was not syndicated in the usual sense, but, since the Courier had fourteen city editions, she was indeed read from coast to coast. Ormes moved to Chicago in 1942. She soon began writing occasional articles for The Chicago Defender, one of the nation's leading black newspapers, a weekly at that time. For a few months at the end of the war, her single panel cartoon, Candy, about an attractive and wisecracking housemaid, appeared in the Defender; the panel ran from March 24 to July 21, 1945

By August 1945, Ormes's work was back in the Courier, with the advent of Patty-Jo 'n' Ginger, a single-panel cartoon which ran for 11 years.[13] It featured a big sister-little sister set-up, with the precocious, insightful and socially politically-aware child as the only speaker and the beautiful adult woman as a sometime pin-up figure and fashion mannequin.

Ormes tackled social and political issues everywhere from race to sex to environmental pollution. In each aspect of her life the cartoonist was involved in humanitarian causes, and her passion for left-wing ideologies post-World War II even led to an investigation by the FBI.

Ormes was posthumously inducted into the National Association of Black Journalists Hall of Fame in 2014,[25] and was inducted into the Will Eisner Comic Industry Eisner Award Hall of Fame as a Judges' Choice in 2018.

Torchy Brown, was appearing in "Dixie to Harlem", 1937.

Will Eisner

This Comic Book is dedicated to a one of the earliest cartoonists to work in the American comic book industry.

Wil Eisner was born on March 6th in 1917 and died on January 3rd, 2005 (aged 87). He was one of the three inaugural inductees to the Will Eisner Comic Book Hall of Fame. The Eisner Award was named in his honor and is given to recognize achievements each year in the comics medium. He was inducted into the Academy of Comic Book Arts Hall of Fame in 1971, and the Jack Kirby Hall of Fame in 1987.

In 1939, Eisner was commissioned to create Wonder Man for Victor Fox, an accountant who had previously worked at DC Comics and was becoming a comic book publisher himself. Following Fox's instructions to create a Superman-type character, and using the pen name Willis, Eisner wrote and drew the first issue of Wonder Comics.

Eisner was drafted into the U.S. Army in "late '41, early '42"[30] and then "had about another half-year which the government gave me to clean up my affairs before going off" to fight in World War II. He was assigned to the camp newspaper at Aberdeen Proving Ground, where "there was also a big training program there, so I got involved in the use of comics for training. ... I finally became a warrant officer, which involved taking a test – that way you didn't have to go through Officer Candidate School.".

On Eisner's return from service and resumption of his role in the studio, he created the bulk of the Spirit stories on which his reputation was solidified. The post-war years also saw him attempt to launch the comic-strip/comic-book series Baseball, John Law, Kewpies, and Nubbin the Shoeshine Boy; none succeeded, but some material was recycled into The Spirit.

The Spirit ceased publishing in 1952. During the 1960s and 1970s, various publishers reprinted the adventures, often with covers by Eisner and with a few new stories from him.

He was inducted into the Academy of Comic Book Arts Hall of Fame in 1971, and the Jack Kirby Hall of Fame in 1987. The following year, the Will Eisner Comic Industry Awards were established in his honor. In 2015, Eisner was posthumously elected to the Society of Illustrators Hall of Fame.

Wow, What a Magazine! No. 3 (Sept. 1936) and The Spirit, Oct 6, 1946..

the U.S. Army publication PS (June 1951) and Comics and Sequential Art hat analyzes the comics medium, published in 1985

Orrin Cromwell Evans

This Comic Book is dedicated to a pioneering African-American journalist and comic book publisher.

Jackie Ormes was born in 1902 and died on August 6th, 1971 (aged 69). He is considered "the first black writer to cover general assignments for a mainstream white newspaper in the United States." he also published All-Negro Comics. the first known comics magazine written and drawn solely by African-American writers and artists. Young Orrin was forced to confront racism at an early age due to his parents' difficult juggling act.

A strong proponent of racial equality, Evans thought he could reach a wider audience with a comic book. When The Record closed after an extended strike action in 1947, Evans partnered with former Record editor Harry T. Saylor, Record sports editor Bill Driscoll and two others to found the Philadelphia publishing company All-Negro Comics, Inc., with himself as president.

In mid-1947, the company published the only known issue of All-Negro Comics, a 48-page, standard-sized comic book with a typical glossy color cover and newsprint interior. The comic's press run and distribution are unknown, and as one cultural historian notes of the era, "While there were a few heroic images of blacks created by blacks, such as the Jive Gray comic strip and All-Negro Comics, these images did not circulate outside of pre-civil rights segregated black communities."

Time magazine in 1947 described the villains in the lead feature, "Ace Harlem," as "a couple of zoot-suited, jive-talking Negro muggers, whose presence in anyone else's comics might have brought up complaints of racial 'distortion.' Since it was all in the family, Evans thought no Negro readers would mind."[1] The protagonist of "Ace Harlem," however, was an African-American police detective; the characters in the "Lion Man and Bubba" feature were meant to inspire black people's pride in their African heritage.

In 1971, shortly before his death, Evans was honored at the annual NAACP convention in Minneapolis and a scholarship was created in his name. In 2014, Evans was elected to the Will Eisner Award Hall of Fame for his work as president of All-Negro Comics.

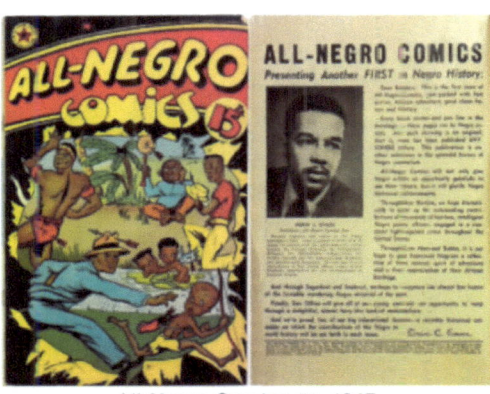

All-Negro Comics #1, 1947

 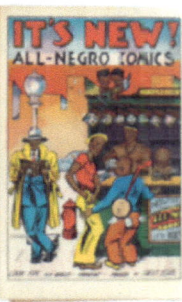

SCOOBI DOGE GAME & MUSIC

Explore the Scoobiverse, build your dreams, groove to Scoobi Doggy Dog on YouTube, and own unique AR NFTs from OpenSea. Join the adventure, expand your horizons!

Source: youtube.com/watch?v=4Zm3UIkYNuU

www.ingramcontent.com/pod-product-compliance
Lightning Source LLC
LaVergne TN
LVHW072310090526
838202LV00018B/2257